to: _Charles_

fROM: _Danny and Mom_

_2021_

gone
fishin'

Published by Sellers Publishing, Inc.
161 John Roberts Road, South Portland, ME 04106
Visit us at www.sellerspublishing.com • E-mail: rsp@rsvp.com

 Like Us on Facebook

Compiled by Robin Haywood.

ISBN-13: 978-1-4162-4534-6

Printed and bound in China.

10 9 8 7 6 5 4 3 2 1

gone fishin'

ARTWORK BY GARY PATTERSON

SELLERS
PUBLISHING

Even a bad day of fishing is better
than a good day at the office.

© GARY & BOB PATTERSON

The way to a man's heart is through his fly.

WHaT I LeaRNeD FRom FiSHiNG:

**Not all good things come
to those who wade.**

**Fishing seems to be
the favorite form of loafing.**

A woman who has never seen her husband
fishing, doesn't know
what a patient man she married.

Fish tremble at the sound of my name.

© GARY PATTERSON

THe THRee RuLeS oF FiSHiNG:

1. Bait your own hook.
2. Clean your own fish.
3. Tell your own lies.

The two best times to fish are when
it's freezin' and when it ain't.

© GARY PATTERSON

WHaT I LeaRNeD FRom FiSHiNG:

Sometimes you really have to squirm to get off the hook.

© GARY PATTERSON

Fishing is a delusion entirely surrounded
by liars in old clothes.

© GARY PATTERSON

Early to bed, early to rise;
fish all day and make up lies.

©GARY PATTERSON

A reel expert can tackle anything.

GARY PATTERSON

A good fisherman knows all the angles.

© GARY PATTERSON

He's not the sharpest hook in the tackle box.

Fish or cut bait . . . !

WHat I LeaRneD FROm FiSHinG:

Even the best lines get weak after
they have been used a few times.

© GARY PATTERSON

Kiss my BASS!

©GARY PATTERSON

Give a man a fish, and you'll feed him for a day. Teach a man to fish, and you get rid of him for the weekend.

If wishes were fishes, we'd have a fish fry.

© GARY PATTERSON

Fishy, fishy in the brook,
get your heinie on my hook!

Fish tales told here.

WHat I LeaRNeD FRom FiSHiNG:

There is no such thing as too much equipment.

All men are equal before fish.

© GARY PATTERSON

A fisherman is a jerk on one end of the line waiting for a jerk on the other.

© GARY PATTERSON

Work is for people who don't know how to fish.

The fishing was good; it was the catching that was bad!

© GARY PATTERSON

I can't wait to get a damn boat!

GARY PATTERSON

Keep the faith and keep fishin'.
It has to get better soon!

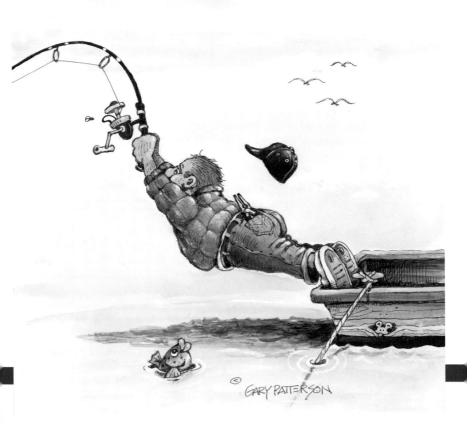

© GARY PATTERSON

Old fishermen never die,
they just smell like they did!

© GARY PATTERSON

WHat I LeaRneD FRom FiSHinG:

The sport of fishing is all about getting outdoors and enjoying life!

©GARY PATTERSON

Credits

p. 10 E. W. Howe; p. 18 Patrick F. McManus; p. 22 Don Marquis;
p. 48 Herbert Hoover